Feeling...
Jealous

First published in 1997
This edition 1999

© Franklin Watts 1997

Franklin Watts
96 Leonard Street
London EC2A 4RH

Franklin Watts Australia
14 Mars Road
Lane Cove
NSW 2006

Series editor: Helen Lanz
Series designer: Kirstie Billingham
Consultant: Anne Peake, Principal Psychologist

A CIP catalogue record for this book
is available from the British Library.

ISBN 0 7496 3565 7

10 9 8 7 6 5 4 3 2 1

Dewey Classification 152.4

Printed at Oriental Press, Dubai, U. A. E.

Feeling...

Jealous

Sally Hewitt

Illustrated by Rhian Nest James

W
FRANKLIN WATTS
LONDON • NEW YORK • SYDNEY

Jack is seven years old. He lives with his mum and dad, his older brother Tom and his little sister Maddie. Usually Jack enjoys playing with his brother and sister, but when Tom or Maddie get all the attention, Jack feels jealous. He wants to shout, "What about ME?"

Do you feel jealous sometimes?

Shilpa is Jack's best friend. She lives with her mum and dad and her little sister Lata.
Jack and Shilpa are in the same class at school. Sometimes Shilpa gets jealous of the other children in her class. When she feels jealous she wants to say horrible things.

What do you do when you feel jealous?

In the morning, Jack's mum dresses his baby sister, Maddie, brushes her hair and gives her breakfast. Mum says Jack is old enough to get ready for school by himself and get his own breakfast. Sometimes he doesn't mind because he likes to make a big bowl of cereal for himself.

He does mind this morning. He feels jealous. He wants Mum to make a fuss of him, not his baby sister. Jack says, "Mum, help me find my library book." Mum says, "Not now Jack, I'm busy. You can do it yourself." "But I want YOU to find it," says Jack and frowns.

Mum can see that Jack feels left out. She stops doing up Maddie's buttons and gives Jack a hug. "We'll find your library book together," she says.

7

On the way to school they meet Shilpa.
She plays peekaboo with Maddie and they
get the giggles. Jack feels left out.
He thinks, "Shilpa is my friend.
She should play with me, not Maddie."

Jack takes Shilpa's hat and puts it on to make her
notice him. Maddie giggles at Jack in Shilpa's hat.
Jack puts Shilpa's hat on Maddie's head and
they all get the giggles. He doesn't feel
left out any more.

When they arrive at school, Jack and Shilpa say goodbye to Maddie. Maddie screams and cries. She doesn't want them to go. Mum says, "Maddie's jealous. She wishes she could go to school, too."

"You can't come, Maddie," says Jack, "you're too little, but I'll play with you when I get home." Maddie stops crying and gives a big smile.

"Come on, Jack," says Shilpa, "we're practising for the play today." Jack feels sorry for Maddie because she can't go with them. But he is glad that he can go to school with Shilpa and his friends.

Jack is playing the drum in the school play.
Shilpa wants to be the dragon. Mr. Davies,
their teacher, says, "Tessie is the dragon.
Shilpa, you can be the rabbit."
"But I want to be the dragon," says Shilpa.
"It's the best part."

Shilpa is very disappointed because she thought Mr. Davies would ask her to be the dragon. She feels jealous of Tessie. She doesn't want Tessie to be the dragon and she doesn't like her any more.

Shilpa is unkind to Tessie. "I would be a much better dragon than you," she says. "Mr. Davies should have given the part to me!" Tessie looks upset.
"You shouldn't boast," says Tona.
"Now you've made Tessie cry," says Billy.

14

Mr. Davies knows that Shilpa is disappointed.
"You'll make a very good rabbit, Shilpa!" he says.
"And Tessie will make a very good dragon."
Tessie wipes her eyes and smiles.

"Everyone has a very important part," says
Mr. Davies. "The princess would never
be rescued if it wasn't for the rabbit."
"And the band wouldn't come in on time
if I didn't play the drum," says Jack.

Shilpa tries on her rabbit costume and begins to feel excited about being the rabbit.
She doesn't mind not being the dragon any more.
She is sorry she was unkind to Tessie.

After school, Shilpa goes back to Jack's house for tea.
Jack's big brother Tom is excited. "Dad's taking
me to a football match for my birthday!" he says.

18

"I want to go!" says Jack.
"You can't! It's my birthday treat, not yours," says Tom.
Jack feels jealous because Dad hasn't given him
a special treat, too. "It's not fair," he says.

Jack wants to spoil his brother's fun.
"I know what Mum and Dad are giving
you for your birthday," says Jack.
"Don't tell me," says Tom. "I want
it to be a surprise."

"Don't spoil Tom's birthday, Jack," says Mum.
"It'll be your birthday soon and then you will
have presents and a special treat of your own."
"And I'll try not to mind if I'm not invited
to come on your special treat," grins Tom.

Dad and Tom set off for the football match.
"Can I go to a football match for my birthday
treat, too?" asks Jack.

22

"Wait and see. It will be a surprise," says Mum. Jack stops feeling jealous of Tom because he and Shilpa are busy wondering what his surprise birthday treat will be.

When Shilpa gets home, her little sister
Lata is wearing her new swimming badge.
"Isn't Lata clever?" says Mum.
"What about me? I've got six swimming
badges," says Shilpa.

Dad is home, too, and he and Mum
make a fuss about Lata's swimming badge.
Shilpa feels jealous. Everyone is praising Lata
and no one is making a fuss about her six
swimming badges!

At bedtime, Shilpa still feels jealous and left out.
She says, "I can swim much better than Lata."

Mum thinks it's Shilpa's turn for some praise.
"Of course you can, you're a very good swimmer,"
she says, "but Lata got her very first badge today."

26

"Do you remember the fuss we made when you got your first badge?" asked Mum. Shilpa laughs. "I even wore my badge to bed, didn't I?"
"I think Lata is still wearing her badge, too," says Mum.

"I wanted you to make a fuss of me,
not Lata," says Shilpa.
"It's very hard not to be jealous
when someone else is getting all
the attention,"says Mum.
"Do you ever feel jealous?"
asks Shilpa.

"Everyone feels jealous sometimes, but I feel much better if I can be happy when other people are happy," says Mum.

"And I feel much better if I think of all the good things that happen to me," says Shilpa.

What do you do to help you to stop feeling jealous?

Notes for teachers and parents

Young children can find it very hard to share. They often want all the attention for themselves. Their feelings of jealousy can make them unhappy and cause them to behave in an unkind and selfish way. Adults and children can find these feelings difficult to understand and discuss.

Sometimes feeling jealous can be understandable, sometimes it can be completely unreasonable. It is important for both adults and children to recognise this feeling, to understand what has generated it and to know how to cope with it. By doing this, strategies can be learned in how to deal with the emotion and what can be done about the situation that caused the feeling of jealousy in the first place.

In the story, Jack and Shilpa are confronted with situations that make them jealous. These incidents can be used as starting points to discuss what can make children feel jealous; they may recognise some of their own behaviour in the story or it may help them to understand the behaviour of others.

The adults in the story provide helpful support for the children. They are used as a way to highlight the reasons behind the jealousy in each situation, providing an insight that children themselves might not be aware of.

The following questions about some of the incidents in the story could be used to generate some discussion.

Further discussion and activities

• On page 7, Jack feels jealous because he wants his mum to make a fuss of him, not his baby sister.

Do you have a little brother or sister? Do you ever feel jealous of them? Why do babies need a lot of attention? How does Mum help Jack to feel better?

• Why does Jack feel left out on page 8? What does he do to stop feeling left out?

• What happened to make Shilpa feel jealous of Tessie on page 13? What does Shilpa do on page 14? Was she right or wrong to do that? Why?

• How does Mr. Davies make everyone feel better on pages 15 and 16?

• Have you ever made someone feel jealous? What did you do? What could you do to help someone to stop feeling jealous of you?

• Do you sometimes say "it's not fair"? Why?

• On page 28, Shilpa and Mum talk about feeling jealous. Everyone feels jealous sometimes. It helps talking to someone you love and trust about how you feel.

It might be helpful to follow up the discussion or story with some activities. Some suggested activities are listed below:

• Make a list of ideas in the book that can help you stop feeling jealous. Which is your favourite idea? You could try it the next time you feel jealous.

• There is a saying, to be "green with envy". Envy is another word for jealous. Draw a picture of someone looking jealous.

• Jack is playing with his new puppy. Shilpa feels jealous. She has always wanted a puppy, but Mum says she can't have one because they haven't got a garden.

Draw a picture or write a story about what happens next to stop Shilpa feeling jealous.

31

Useful words

to boast
Boasting is when you tell someone how clever you are or that you are really good at doing something and you don't care what the other person thinks.

disappointed
A feeling you can get when something doesn't turn out as well as you wanted it to, or when you feel let down.

excited
You can feel excited when you are looking forward to something nice that is going to happen. When you are excited you might feel like laughing and jumping about.

to feel left out
You can feel left out when nobody notices you and nobody asks you to join in the fun.

to feel sorry for
You can feel sorry for someone when they are upset and you understand just how they feel. You want to help them to feel better again.

getting attention
You are getting attention when people are making a fuss of you and are interested in what you are doing.

jealous
A feeling you get when everyone is making a fuss of someone else and nobody is taking any notice of you.

to praise
This is when someone notices that you have done a good job, or that you have been kind or helpful, and says "well done!". When someone praises you, it makes you feel pleased and proud of yourself.

to spoil something
This is when someone ruins something on purpose that someone else is doing. For example, if you are drawing a picture and someone scribbles on it, that person has spoilt your picture.